Paper Boats

Merasen-na Jamir

 pencil

ISBN 978-93-5458-925-6

© Merasen-na Jamir 2021

Published in India 2021 by Pencil

A brand of

One Point Six Technologies Pvt. Ltd.

123, Building J2, Shram Seva Premises,

Wadala Truck Terminal, Wadala (E)

Mumbai 400037, Maharashtra, INDIA

E connect@thepencilapp.com

W www.thepencilapp.com

Author biography

Merasen-na Jamir is twenty-three years old and is currently pursuing her Msc In Counselling Psychology. She is also the author of the book, *Into My Abyss* which was published in the year 2020. Apart from writing stories, she shares a deep love for poetry. She considers writing poems as an art of expressing herself. Apart from publishing and posting her poems on Wattpad, *Paper Boats* is her first poetry book that has a variety of poems as random as it's title.

CONTENTS

Eleven January

If forever doesn't reach this life,

I will keep loving you now.

As the creator made you,

Beautifully flawed in so many parts,

I still love you.

And I hope tomorrow I still will.

To live through the good in your good morning wishes,

To stay safe in your take care messages as I leave home.

To let go of the times when you roast me,

To keep balance with your silence.

Teaching me I need not apologise for everything.

For praising God together with me.

For never complaining even when you have a lot
to.
And I'd like to be realistic,
If tomorrow pulls you away from me,
Gives me the greatest heartbreaks of all times,
I still will sing praises of your being.
For you gave me the courage to write about love
again.

All The Things We Did

Haven't we all begged a piece of shit to stay? Not that they are bad people but they chose to be cruel to us at that time we met and knew them. Haven't we loved intensely to the point that they were actually the ones who taught us more about self-love ? Haven't we all thought that, that was the end of us as a person and love as a feeling? Haven't we all loved someone so undeserving yet with all of the made up atoms we are? Not that they don't deserve love, just that they did not deserve ours. Yet, here we are with lessons embodied in us about how a devastating experience can build an entire empire called You.

And we will live life, be happy, grateful, and find love with the one who knows how to love each part of it.

I Will Love You Till The Last Point

Dear Mrs Beaver, I am young but my hands are turning cold,

Little flakes of loneliness is what I saw in place of snow.

In time your eyes will slowly turn from green to gold,

Will the frostbites numb me or will it be my fairest foe?

In this voluminous suffering, we are alone yet together.

For we both feel pain, mild to intense we all do.

We groan with thoughts combined with this displeasure,

Yet love is love; Fresh waters in green to salt waters in blue.

From human to human,
To living to moving,
To walking to flying,
From cell to cell- each feels.

From each drop of water to every grain of sand;
Someone will always love you till the departed land.

Romance

If you haven't ever seen snow, I am telling you someday you will or I will bring it to your grave. I promise. You sip your coffee even when you are alone and you feel satisfied, you don't need the whole world to tell you that you have to sit and drink your caffeine with someone else. You can dance around all by yourself and you don't need someone to hold your hand because romanticising isn't always about lovers. Love starts with you. experience everything you find joy in, by yourself or together and the rest will follow.

My Art

Loving him is like Christmas. The warmth that my heart feels. It is all the lights that make the city look cozy as it reflects in my eye. It is the hot delicious coffee that I sip to soothe my body from the cold. It is feeling fuzzy in my red sweater as I hug my animal soft doll. It is like sitting around the fireplace with my family. Love is when I feel safe with being who I am with him. Love is when he is unapologetically himself with me. Yet some years it may be cold and hard as it passes, and that is exactly what loving him is like. Heart-aching sometimes yet I know how much value gratitude and love it carries every single time because all year long I wait for it to be thankful for the miracle.

Love and Losing

It's like when you wake up thirsty in the middle of the night and you find a bottle with the right amount of water to quench your thirst. Like sitting on your balcony on a rainy day with a cup of coffee with your favorite music. When you rush to the hospital all worried, and the doctor says, *"It's alright now,"* . Like how a warm ginger and honey tea could relieve your sore throat. When you feel exhausted and take a lukewarm bath, all the aches seem to disappear. Like hearing all your favorite hellos all at once. That's how love finds its way in even when it is hurting. Imagine losing all of that all at once.

A Fall of Grace

Even when the sky melts my heart away,

If it could be presented to me, I don't want it.

Nights where the moonlight shines on me or,

If you could give me the sun yet I'd stay still.

When the shadows try to devour me whole or,

When my feet walked deeper than the depth of the

ocean

Still I stood and I thought I would stand forever

But when His Grace touched me,

I started shaking not terrified but overwhelmed,

And how I fell all at once on my knees,

And how relieved I was that I did.

Summer Child

Beware of the child you met in Summer's bloom

You shall see her kindness in glory,

Of the leaves that carry tremendous storms.

The child no longer hides when it rains,

Dancing to the droplets, she welcomes winter.

Beware of the child you saw in Summer's bloom,

Once the child who prayed to hold tight,

Has now learnt to pray to let go.

Almost

I sit on the chair we usually keep outside in the veranda. The breeze eases me from all the heat I felt in the afternoon. Sometimes it rains hard as if it roars for fall to come sooner because as soon as it stops, it gets colder. The green leaves are starting to turn honey brown yet they haven't fallen yet. At night it's almost as if it's the coming of a new season but the crickets still sing throughout the dark. This is how it's almost, almost there. How I think I almost miss home but I am at home where I am. Almost at the point of loving him with all I can but there's room for more. How I think I am almost not human but I still have it in me. Always almost towards the end but I am right where I need to be.

I Love You The Most

Despite what I do and how I live, I always love You the most.

It's the kind of love I cannot explain because with every tenth breath I take, I hurt You.

If disappointment came in packages, I would still bring You a load.

I am tired of the way I treat You but I cannot stop.

Ashamed inside a cocoon of lies and manipulations.

There isn't really a need for a court to pass it's ruling, You and I both know the guilt I carry.

Yet You always carry it for me when it's too heavy for me.

Yet You choose me over anything and everything.

Yet You listen to what I have to say and probably nod along.

You believe in me more than I could believe in You or myself.

You teach and taught me a lot yet I keep throwing it away.

You hand me joy, one that I cannot find anywhere.

And with everything I am, You still believe me when I say I love you.

I wonder how many tears You shed every passing minute.

But I know how much blood You gave up for someone like me,

So, despite what I do and how I live, I will always love You the most.

Rest

Today I feel physically tired. It's awful when your body can hurt so much but it is also satisfactory when the pain comes from something positive. So I thought if I fell down a fresh green mountain right now, I would surrender and roll down calmly. This is when I realised that I need to give in to the pain and accept it at times. Why do I need to complain about a situation that will **eventually** end when it is time. That I should let things flow as it is when I am tired. That **not** every**thing requires me to exhaust myself** more than I can handle.

Questions

A lot of times you will find yourself asking questions to other people whose answers don't necessarily add to you. You keep asking them, *Do you like me? Do you hate me? Are you mad at me? Did I hurt you? Are you leaving me?* But never will you ever ask questions that matter to you. I am no better than you, so here I go. I want to ask myself, *what is the most beautiful thing about me?* Maybe it is loving in depth even when I know there is a risk of losing so much. Maybe it's the way I carry myself. Though most of the time I lose silently, it never defeats me. Maybe it's the way I try to love myself even when it's so hard to. Maybe it's the forgiveness I carry like an endless fountain. Maybe it's all the things I will ask myself without any apologies.

You Are Not A Half

Often what you do out of love isn't wrong. It's what you choose not to do for yourself. A part of you stretches way beyond the sea when you choose to let go piece by piece. And sometimes you cannot bring those pieces back together because you choose to shatter over the same thing over and over again. It becomes too small to be fitted back in. So you have to remind yourself that loving can be in different forms and sometimes letting go completely is one. Because at the end of the day all the love you freely give can come back to you, but what will you do with it all if you have none left for yourself? Remember no one is your other half. **You are not the other half, You are the whole.**

If It Is Poetry

I don't care about so many things and care so much about other things too. This is not a paradox, sometimes it is called being who we are as humans. People ask me how I can forgive easily, I ask myself that too. Yet when I am all alone sitting with my vulnerability I say that, people too need to be forgiven because I too am forgiven. Because in my forgiveness is a part of pain I have felt some time in life. Because I try so hard to be good sometimes, it makes me sick and break somewhere inside me. But then I tell myself that carrying around this weight of being too nice of a human is a sin in itself. How I run back and forth as if this life of mine is a cinderella movie. In those moments I tell myself there will be cloudy days because I am living. And in those days when I meet people, I don't want to know what your instagram is, I don't want to socialise. I want to know about what inspired you to live and be alive even when you and I became nothing and everything.

L

When you wear a ring and it doesn't fit you, what
do you do?

You take it off.

When you apply something and your body is
allergic to it, what do you do?

You cleanse it off.

When you wear a shirt but it makes you
uncomfortable, what do you do?

You change into something else.

When your phone is unrepairable what do you do?

You try to get a new phone.

You liked the ring you had,

You invested time applying,

The shirt cost you a lot,

It takes time to get a new phone but you eventually
you do,
So what do you do when someone is hurting, being
toxic, makes you uneasy or damages you?
You freely let them go, for your betterment.
It's hard but you need to remove them.

Break Wholly

Every morning you tell yourself to try,

Every night you are tired of breaking,

Crying and soaking yourself away in thoughts,

My dear, I want to ask, "Why are you so scared of

breaking?"

Who told you that was wrong?

You worked yourself so hard all along,

You cannot stay there comfortably warm all your

life,

You have to break out of your cocoon to witness

your flight.

So please break apart every piece that holds you

back from letting you out and break wholly.

Greet Your Past And Be Friends With It

That wholly untold story of yours? Yeah, that one where you told bits and parts of it to some people, but couldn't bring yourself to tell the entire thing?

Yes. That's the past, you and I, we all have.

The only thing that separates us is the notion that we think we are alone in this.

It's a graveyard to you and you're scared that the ghost of what's gone is going to haunt you.

But you know, if your past is filled with graves, make that damn thing into a garden.

Be someone who can walk up there and see the beauty and identify yourself as part of that beauty.

The goal here is not to forget your past, not to accept that it was rotten or that it is dead, or not about letting go.

If you do that, I'm afraid you'll never succeed at it.

Because I know of it. Have seen it and tried it out.

And I too, have made a sad graveyard of all the files and bodies from the past.

And now I know that I can only turn those bodies into fertilizers to grow my own garden with the seeds of the flowers that I love.

That the ultimate and only way is to be able to walk right back and be okay with seeing those parts that left.

To no longer feel it's chains, to no longer be a prisoner of my own paradise.

It will not shiver me, it will no longer control me.

And I will simply stand there gazing at it's beauty unfazed because I will make a home out of it that radiates light.

And you and I, and everyone of us will get there someday.

The Self Love We Talk About

And when the universe asks you what is love,

Do not dare to define it with the love you feel,

Do not give it a form out of the what others give
you,

Your lover may have swam the deepest oceans for
you,

Your mother may have shown you the purest that
is,

But you shall never know of it's value if you do not

define it for yourself.

If everything starts with us, it starts with you.

Everything Belongs In Me

I've been questioned a lot of times,

What do you write about?

Which do you love the most?

Why do you speak of sadness then turn to happiness?

Let it transcend to pain, transform it to power and then talk about breaking down?

How do you think a man feels, and scribbles down the heart of a woman?

Where does your mind usually stay and then continue with the flow of your heart?

I shall cease to exist in everything I feel and witness.

For you see, I don't belong anywhere but everything belongs in me.

Home

I have to stay still and not move to let the pain subside. I think of Mama and what she would do for me, had she been here. She told me she has a mild cold so I can't call her. I want her to rest as well. Some say home is where you are, while some say home is the people you love. Yet Home is never just one. There are many homes we build as we go. In small towns, tiny spaces, narrow roads, somewhere vast and big, and mostly in the treasured pieces of our hearts where people stay. Home is in the hug I share with Mama, in the laughs I have with Dad, in the small talks with my brother, in the car rides when he picks me up, in the play and self talk with my pets, in the silly chatters with my cousins, in the adventures with my friends, in my heart I carry. **Home is evrywhere and each leaves you with a longing.**

Puzzle

Dismantling pieces of your whole self does not mean you are weak. Sometimes what looks fixed does not actually make it work right. Just because you thought it was the right order and looks well fitted does not mean it is. This is not your destruction but your evolution. Healing means understanding that growth takes place in forms that may be unfavorable. If it requires you to assemble all the puzzle pieces from scratch then so be it.

Still You Do

Just like the sun shines, so do you.

Every single day you rise up despite the night,

Every single day you shine despite the rain.

On days when it is cloudy you shy away but you

come back stronger.

If I could, I would look at you daily,

But how can a mere human look at you?

You seem so far away and full of power,

Sometimes out of my reach and I feel like I'm

lonely,

And each time I feel dejected because of it,

You look at me and fill my day with warmth.

How wonderful marvellous of a woman you are,

To be compared to the sun and still it isn't enough,

Still you shine the brightest my dear.

Collections Of Grace

I questioned His love and waged a war against
Him,
Everybody left for home while He stood.
"Why?" I asked,
*"I never leave the one that needs saving more than the
ninety nine that's saved,"* He replied.

Do You ask This When You Try To Sleep

What was it for all of us really?

- Was it not being able to walk on water? Or was it the feeling of drowning on land? Was it knowing that the definition of beauty was wholly wrong because gardens were only considered pretty when roses and colourful flowers bloomed? Tell me what was it that drew us all closer to the edge? Was it the fear of falling or was it us **(you)**?

This Is To Drown

I thought of a lot of things one after another. Like trying to catch the sound of ripples, desperately trying to ignite a fire when it is pouring and your body feels as if it's giving up because of the cold. As you wait for me for an answer, I can't do this I guess. The best I could say was, *"If we wonder how the color blue would taste like if it were edible, would it taste like stale bubblegum, or another flavour of cola? Or maybe mint? We can never be sure,"*

So I don't know what it would feel to let go of people I love to let them find happiness.

Things We never Ask

Time and time again I think, are you sad? Or are you obsessed over being sad? Have you been sad for so long that you no longer welcome anything that isn't gloomy because it's an emotion you aren't familiar with? Sometimes things are long gone but we built a home out of all these places that we no longer allow anything other than what makes us comfortable. So are you sad because you don't authorise yourself to feel happy?

In Gratitude

But even when it hurt, it always made sure to let me know of it's presence. Some days it would drizzle lightly, from the morning till the day's end. Sometimes it would make loud roars and strike even when nobody could see it, because it was during the day as if it were angry on my behalf. Some nights it would give me a calm aura with a gentle breeze as though it was it's way of calming me down. How could I forget how on some days, it would just shine bright, telling me that there is a much more glorious life than the gloomy days I will experience. I am certain when I talk to all these moments, it is not just I, but us collectively feeling the same. This intense bubble of wholesomeness we feel out of gratitude towards the Sky that takes care of us even when nobody notices.

Everything Everything

We are treated otherwise just because we were born with different genitals,

But how do I accept love from a race that does horrendous acts on animals?

Judged because the way you love is different,

Given a certain degree of value because of the colour of your skin.

Turned a blind eye on places that need help,

Sit idle while there are forests burning.

How can I trust a race that shoots like it's second nature?

That rejects the law of its own race because someone has money power all over.

That considers borders and territories much more important than living in peace.

In times of a world pandemic that is taking away millions of lives, online studying is compulsory because the future of children is more important than some unfortunate man's daily bread and butter.

A degree is way more valuable than the lives of thousands.

That denies that there is suffering and that we are slowly transforming into monsters of the most menacing kind.

A race that breaks each other apart.

A race that chooses to reciprocate hate with hate.

This is Everything, Everything I want to spit on one.

What We Owe Ourselves

I too have died like you, a lot of times. I don't know how many parts of me I have killed but it doesn't hurt anymore. They say in Spring you bloom, in Summer you thrive, in Fall you break down, and in Winter you wither away. Yet no one talked about how it was in mid Summer, when we laid awake as we greeted the ghosts of the ones we killed last May. The seasons of our growth were all jumbled up and incorrect with the weather of the Earth. For none has talked about it, but it was during Fall that gave birth to the brightest version of me, and in the cold winter none of the frostbite could numb me anymore. The Earth is a place that gives me home and I(We), someone to keep it occupied so that it isn't alone. So you see, no matter how many times you fall as long as you want to stand up, the Earth will grant you the strength to kill all the versions of you, you need to leave behind. So be merciless but embrace it.

Γυναίκα

I know we are fragile,

For we carry so much love.

Yes, in the wrong hands, we do tend to break

But each time it is without the need of a man that

we repair ourselves.

Like the different Seven Mighty Seas,

Please find beauty in our seven personalities that

would be empty if one disappears,

I know sometimes it is extremely frustrating to

figure us out,

We say some things and mean the opposite of it,

For we do not want to demand attention from you.

Our circuits tend to blow and we scream at times,

And this is not an excuse but the mere truth;

We were born destined to carry the weight of own worlds.

Be easy on us though we are confusing,

We do not wish to be like that at all,

But we were made this way.

We are women, so complicated and like the biggest jigsaw puzzle,

Because the end portrait is that we are a vast galaxy of endless love, care and pour.

So much that often we tend to love you more than the love we give ourselves,

And you ask, and we ask- why do we break so hard?

This is not a verse to say we are above you,

But a note to understand us even a bit better.

Learn to accept us the way we were created and we will evolve even greater,

And if you cannot, though the bidding may be harsh, we shall learn to grow, go on, accept ourselves without you.

This is who we are; Women.

If You Are Empty

I stared at the ventilation and tried to reach my mind, but all I noticed along with the sound of raindrops and soundless lightning flashes was how empty things can seem sometimes. Emptiness is something you and I both have and can feel. Five years back in time, I would have been terrified. It isn't because I am older now nor is it because I grew through experiences. It is more in the downright silence of the erie emptiness that I found that it was lovely. Who ever said that being empty does not make you whole? When did we make it seem unacceptable for us to be bare? **Emptiness** isn't a worthless vacant spot, it is a space that you have the power to fill with anything you want.

Compass

Drilled with holes on every edge,

You fear I might die.

My dear that's where my light comes in,

And how all my poison goes out.

There are so many strokes on me

So you call me a masterpiece,

But I'm just Vegvisir.

Dead Men Tell No Tales

We have long heard and believed, *dead men tell no tales*

Yet as the flames go up and the waves rise, everything wails.

We never murdered her, she did the deed to herself

There's more to time than clocks counting to twelve.

Neither am I God nor the devil to give ample chances,

Massacring every hue with a game of masquerade

Like strings attached unto minds everybody dances,

Ballistically the show will transcend to a ballet.

You begin bleeding, then pleading for sheathing.

Weren't you fine, when you defined what was divine?

Weren't you acting for a life everlasting, now you are unmasking ?

Now I am asking if we are recasting the king?

When all joy is lost and your merry comes to an end,

You pretend to bend and blend and never be condemned.

Dead men tell no tales, you breathe and breed hate,

Cerberus was never killed, only returned to Hades.

Please

Please don't be out there in this already deranged world trying to put someone down. Please don't place all of your power into judging someone you don't know any better than yourself. Everybody has it hard. Some people realise their weaknesses and some just haven't seen their flaws yet. This does not mean you have the right to grant judgement over the blind. Please choose to seek, love, grow, and lend a hand when given the chance. Please do not be out here justifying your righteousness when you choose to be toxic instead of love. This isn't about forgiving people, this is about us trying to be human. This is about not letting hate, pride, and disgust win.

Perhaps

Perhaps I think, for perhaps it is only what I can say sometimes. Had I stood in front of the ocean, and the receding waves touched my feet, perhaps I would feel all the life underneath the water. It will not come to my mind that I cannot swim, nor that I have a phobia for water. Because all I shall ever see is how big and vast the ocean is and how this mighty wholeness is kissing my feet. And how I could break it's stillness if I wished. About how it reflects half of the beautiful sky but all it can do is watch me from above, because it cannot reach out to me. I hope that in that moment, I will know how small my being is yet I have power over everything because I can move at my will.

Paper Boats

There is hurricane inside a part of me,

There is a desert in another.

Light drizzles and storms in some parts,

Another witnesses a drought.

Famine, tsunamis and cyclones.

And you ask me what exactly am I?